DIMENSIONAL-ISM
BY KEITH APPLEBY
REVISION 2 (2022)

PREFACE 3
4TH DIMENSION 11
THE SPIRIT WORLD 16
THE HUMAN BODY 21
THE DREAM WORLD 28
SPIRITUALISTS AND MEDIUMS 35
SPIRITS AND TIME 41
MY HISTORY 45
DISABILITIES AND SPIRTS 52
COMMUNICATION WITH SPIRTS 55
MEDIATION 61
GHOST HUNTS AND THE LIKE 65
MY PLANS AND GOALS 71
HOW YOU CAN HELP 78
REFERENCES 80

CHAPTER ONE
Preface

Firstly I would like to thank you for your interest in my book, and my thoughts and feelings within the world of spiritualism and I hope you enjoy reading this document as much as I have enjoyed writing it. This book contains my personal beliefs and is not a factual account of what is true or not.

My name is Keith Robert Appleby, I am 46 years old as of writing this book, and live in the North East of England and other than having a bachelors degree within the field of TV & Film production, I am nothing special, however I do have a very logical, strange and somewhat imaginary mindset due to having Autistic traits and have suffered from what I can only explain as spiritual activity for most of my life. Some say that I have a childish mind, which could help to explain some of my life experiences.

The information I have placed in this book, is from my own personal experiences, including my own logical thoughts and beliefs on the world of spiritualism. Everything that I write herein, is always done so in the logical manner, using the information that I have available. If something cannot be proven or physically observed by my own eyes I do not believe it or trust it.

I want to make it clear from the start of this book, that I am in the most circumstances a spiritualist, however I do not follow the general routines and church visits, I do not believe in "the Light" as I do not believe in a God, or for that matter a Devil. My experience as well as my intellect have allowed me to create and envisage my own version of spiritualism, which I have generally dubbed "Dimensional-ism". As you will see from the contents of this book, my ideas have a lot of similarities to spiritualism, however there is on big significant difference. There is no mention of a Devine spirit and all of what I state is either provable of from my own experiences, which unfortunately at this moment is not provable. As the saying goes, the best evidence is what you witness yourself.

This book is written in order to provide you the reader with my thoughts and thought process, with regards to the world of spirits, how I believe it works, how and why we can or cannot see them, or hear them, and how we interact with the spirit world. I would like to indicate that when I mention the spirit world, I am actually talking about the 4th dimension. I will explain this in a later chapter.

One of the questions you may be asking yourself, is what sort of skills or qualifications do I have, that would give me an authority on this matter, when of course, there are many individuals who, with an education and legitimate spiritual qualifications have stated otherwise? And in response to that question, the only possible answer I can provide is through experience and actual involvement within the spirit world, as well as the evidence that I have seen, although that does not justify your need for evidence. As many people will attest to, qualifications mean nothing, its experience that is a deciding factor and as such I am one of the foremost figures available to make these statements.

Yes that is right! I have experience in the spirit world. I have spoken with spirits. I have seen spirits. I have been attacked by spirits all through my life from birth, and on top of this I have also spoken to an individuals who were not capable of speech.

Let me provide you with an example and explanation of that last comment, so that you can understand what I mean.

In 1993 at the age of 17, I began working here in the UK through the government on an apprenticeship scheme. They were great avenues into full time employment at one time, however they hardly exist these days. I arranged and began working in a nursery school for children between the age of 3 and 4. these children only stayed at the school for half a day.

Once a week, a local disability school would bring disabled children to the nursery to enable them to become accustomed to other children, and on this particular day they had brought two children with them, a boy aged 5, who was confined to a wheelchair and a girl aged 7. I was not aware at the time that the little girl was unable to speak. I cannot remember the reason but, it was this little girl that had an actual conversation with me.

On the morning of the visit a child (or at least I believe it was a child you will see why later) had stuffed toilet paper into the plug hole of one of the sinks, and had turned the taps on full. The bathroom, which was a large room with around 8 toilets and 8 sinks, flooded with water everywhere. One of the children in the nursery told me about the incident and led me into the bathroom. I turned off the tap and began to usher all the children out of the room, or at least I thought I had.

I removed the toilet tissue from the plug to allow the water to drain out of the sink, and as I was doing so, I began to mumble to myself, which is something I tend to do when I'm frustrated or annoyed. Suddenly from behind me I hear a voice, a little girl said "It wasn't me." I turned around to find the little girl from the visiting school standing next to the bin. I thought I had removed all the children for safety reasons, but It appeared that I had not. I had not seen her, and when I heard her voice, that was when I realised she was still in the room

With a calm, sweet voice, I replied to the girl as she was looking at me "I know sweetheart, Come on lets get out of here" and I slowly walked her out of the room, retrieved the mop and bucket and returned to clean the mess that was now covering the floor.

It was later in the day, after filling in the required report card, that I was called back to the headmasters office, to be informed that I could not possibly have heard this young girl, as she could not speak. Now I am fully aware of something called selective mutism, however this girl had additional issues, which selective mutism would not cover. They never explained as to why she couldn't talk, just that she couldn't, and I never thought to enquire.

I was confused, but did not really think anything about it, and just wrote it off as a mistake until a later date, when addition strange unusual voices echoed throughout my ears, that could not have possibly been legitimate. One of which was that of a seven month old baby girl stating that she needed to poop, and seconds later began to fill her nappy.

Lots of other situations have led me to believe that it may be possible that I have some sort of telepathic ability. However only if I am not looking at the subject and do not know of any possible reason for them not being able to speak.

It is also my belief that telepathic abilities are not solely for humans, as such I believe it is also possible to speak to animals telepathically, let me explain why; Many years ago, I did attend a church for spiritualists and it was during one of these evenings that I noticed a small dog, running around the room. It would run up to me and then run to another individual. I never said anything about it, but four days later that same little dog turned up in my bedroom, waking me from sleep, with its bark. I knew the dog was a Yorkshire terrier and someone or something then spoke the word "Whiskey" which I immediately assumed was the dogs name. The dog would not let me sleep, until I had basically said aloud "OK, I will let her know." at that point, the dog disappeared. That weekend the same dog reappeared at the church running between me and this other woman so, when I had the opportunity, I approached the lady and explained what had happened to me.

To begin with, I asked the lady if she knew of a Yorkshire terrier by the name of Whiskey, to which she replied yes. I told her that it was here, at this moment, When I told her that it was here she burst into tears. Her beloved dog had only passed over about 3 weeks prior and all the details matched. Once again I got a name (you will see why I say this in another section)

We are taught at an early age that voices come from the mouth, as such we look for a moving mouth to realise that someone is talking. However, if the mouth is not moving then we do not associate any noise coming from that individual. Look at a ventriloquist such as Jeff Dunham. When you watch his show, although, we know that Jeff is the one that is talking, his mouth does not move, which gives us the impression that the dummy is speaking. We also know from experience that animals cannot talk.

I want to task you with a test. If you go on you tube and watch a video of Jeff Dunham live at home, he is speaking into the camera, but his mouth hardly moves. You start to believe that he cannot possibly be talking. Let me explain. If you cannot see the mouth moving you do not associate the sound with that mouth. It is strange to watch Jeff Dunham live. Due to the years of training his mouth hardly moves, even when talking normally. It would be impossible to lip read.

This I believe to be much the same situation with ourselves. If we can see the mouth is not moving then our minds are set to a state of nothing. However, if we cannot see the mouth, and we can hear speech we can often assume that the individual is talking to us without evidence to back it up.

Does that mean that people are capable of telepathy and just do not realise it? I believe that there must be some certain requirements, for example that we must not be able to associate voice with the movement of mouth. In all cases of me hearing voices from individuals or from out of the ether I have never been looking at anyone directly, however they have been the only individual in the location.

Is it possible that even when a child or adult cannot speak, they can speak through telepathy, and as humans can we be capable of hearing them? This questions has forced me to think through my religious beliefs very closely and as such come to the conclusions that I am covering within this book.

My logic predicts a simple explanation to all of this, and this book will I hope help you to understand the basis behind my beliefs and how it is possible that we can communicate with each other without the need of voice.

This book will also cover many aspects of the spiritual world, and how my thought processes have been directed to the decisions I have taken with regards to my beliefs. It will explain why I believe the fourth dimension is the spirit world, why we sometimes can and cannot see spirits, why we can and cannot hear spirits. We will cover information about our brains, and what our brains are for and what I believe they do. We will cover subjects in this book such as the dream world, lucid dreaming and how it all connects to spirits that are on the earth.

I have spoken with many people, friends and family about my thoughts as well as discussing with other people on the internet, and in all circumstances intrigued them with the information I am bout to give you. With many people asking questions which I have been able to answer with ease. I hope that my thoughts and ideas help you to feel better about your beliefs.

I want to point out that I am a very sceptical individual and as such, evidence is a prime requirement for me to believe in anything, as such I don't believe in god, as there is no evidence to prove that a god exists and although I respect other peoples' opinions, the lack of evidence does not prove the contrary. As such my beliefs are all based on logical evidence that can be backed up by either research or personal experience in the matter.

Again I wish to thank you greatly for reading this book, and I hope that I can give you an impressive insight into the spiritual world and the connection it has to the human world or that of the third dimension.

CHAPTER TWO

The 4th dimension

I want to start by talking about the 4th dimension, what is it and how it works. The world as we know it is made up of three dimensions, they are allocated as length, breadth and height, this allows us to see items in what we know as three dimensional. Everything we deal with on a daily basis has these three properties.

As 3d objects we can look into and manipulate any 2d object, for example pictures, films, TV programs. These are all 2d objects that we can interact with without any issues, however, we cannot interact with the 4th dimension in the same way, we can only see or interact with a minute part of that dimension at any one moment.

In order to explain this in better details, we need to step down a dimension, and imagine we are living and surviving in the 2nd dimension. By doing so we will be able to understand what I mean with regards to the interaction with the 4th dimension.

Within the 2nd dimension we will only have access to length and breadth, as height does not exist, as such we loose the ability to see in 3d.

So, understanding this we need to take a 3d object, let us take this image of a football as an example

as you can clearly see, it is a football, this is because of the 3rd dimension. We can see the height, breadth and length of the object however if we take a look at this football from within the second dimension, we would not realise it is a football, as we would only see the equivalent of:

As you can see from the above image, it is not possible for us to determine what this object is. However, what we can do as 3rd dimensional beings is interact by moving the two dimensional aspect of view. For example, we can move the image down or up.

In all circumstances as a 2d creature we can only see a part of the 3d object. We can not see as a two dimensional being see the whole object, and we cannot move the view we can see. Only interaction from a 3rd dimensional being can manipulate that for us.

I can imagine you are now asking what this has to do with the 4th dimension, well as I have explained with regards to the 2nd dimension, we as beings from that dimension we can see, but not alter the following dimension. For example, we cannot go up or down, so cannot see the full object. A higher dimension must move us for that to happen as such we can look at the 3rd dimension and 4th dimension in the same way.

As 3d beings we interact with the 4th dimension in some way, however we cannot control that 4th dimension, as such the question remains, what is the 4th dimension?

Plenty of research is available on the internet regarding the 4th dimension, but I want to break this down as much as I can. If we start at the bottom of the ball in the 2d world and go up, the ball will grow then shrink again.

A great video explaining this can be found on you tube at the following address:

https://www.youtube.com/watch?v=eGguwYPC32I&t=3s

The same principle exists in the 3rd dimension. To us an object from the 4th dimension would grow and then shrink again. There are videos on the internet on you tube referring to this and explaining how it works. So, the question here is how can we explain this? What is it, in the 3rd dimension that grows and shrinks? And how does the 4th dimension effect that growth and shrinkage.

The answer is quite simple, what in the 3rd dimension grows, and shrinks? The answer is living matter. For example, Humans, animals, plants, trees and so forth. Everything grows, then rots and shrinks, but the question still remains, what effects the growth and shrinkage, and the answer is quite simple. "Time".

Time is the factor that we are looking for. Over time we grow from a baby, into an adult, and then shrink as we get older. The same can be said of animals and plants. Time produces growth and shrinkage. And just like the 2nd Dimension cannot make any modifications to the height of an object as they cannot see the whole, we as 3d beings cannot manipulate time. As we cannot see the whole of it, we are forced to flow through time at specific intervals (what we consider as seconds).

As such it is therefore logical to assume that the 4th dimension is itself, time. Many scientists believe that the 4th dimension is called "space time", however I am not totally convinced, unless they are classing space time as a unit of time, and not a unit of area as well as time, which to me is what it sounds like.

One additional item I want to point out is that a 2d being can see us, if we are in their line of view. However, they will as with the ball only see part of us, and not all of us. As such it is possible for the 2nd dimension being to actually see a 3d dimensional being, but only for a minute amount.

The above statement only works if we as a 3d being are in the line of sight of that 2d being, you will see why I make this statement in a later chapter, as it falls in with the explanation of being in the right place at the right time.

CHAPTER THREE
The spirit world

Based on the above we have now established the 4th dimension is time, so how does that interact with the spirit world. It is my belief that spirits are just us living within the 4th dimension. When we die our body releases the spirit into the 4th dimension and that is where we live for a long period of time.

Many people claim to have seen or heard spirits, but many are sceptical because not everyone sees spirits. Can this be explained? I believe it can and I will attempt to do so below

Firstly, We need to look at the aspect of time in our world, we work in seconds, however with the technology we have we can now dissect a second into at least five millionths of a second (a 5ghz computer for example can count up to 5 million in one second).

I believe that spirits like us have full access to the dimension they are in. we can see all of the height, as such I believe that spirits can see all of time, or at least all of time from the moment we are deceased (I will explain this later)

There needs to be several criteria met for us to see spirits, these include, the spirit being able to control their own choices (I will explain this in further chapter as well). We need to be paying attention and in explaining that, I mean we need to be looking in the right place at the right time.

If you take into consideration that we are in a certain time frame at any given second, a spirit would also need to be within that time frame in order for us to see them. As spirits have roam of all time, then the actual chances of seeing a spirit are extremely rare, as the spirit would need to be in that time frame at the same moment we ourselves are in the same time frame. It is hard to explain, however remember what I said earlier regarding a 2d being seeing us, we would have to be in their line of sight. I would suggest if you wish to understand what I mean then I would watch a film called "the Langoliers" by Stephen king. This film demonstrates the process of my thoughts. Or even "The Others" which is another great film that somewhat demonstrates my point.

Now let me explain It this way. I have already said that we can break a second down to almost 5 million tick (a count to 1 is classed as 1 tick, as a 5ghz computer can count to 5 million, that would be 5 million ticks in one second), so let us assume that a spirit is sat in the 4th Dimension. As we pass through that second, we will only see that spirit when we are in exactly that same tick. The spirit will not exist in any other ticks that the one in which they are sat, as such there is a great possibility that we will not see it. That would mean that there is a 1 in 5 million chance or a 0.0000005% chance we would see a spirit in that second.

However, our eyesight is not that perfect and we cannot distinguish that sort of data in a second. As such the chances of us actually seeing a spirit is extremely rare as a spirit would need to span through several hundred thousand ticks in order for us to see them. We have scientific proof that we can distinguish between 150 and 250 images a second. Transferring that into our 5 million ticks a spirit would need to be present for 20 thousand ticks, for us to even see a glimpse of that spirit (that would be 1 of those 250 images for the best of eyes per second), that would be the equivalent of you standing still for 20 thousand seconds or 333 minutes or five and a half hours. and if you consider the fact that we have four directions we can examine that and that will narrow the possibilities even more. Just with 5 million ticks and the direction we now have 390 billion in 1 chance of seeing a spirit. That is only if the spirit appears for 1 of those 250 images (which to tell you the truth you probably wouldn't see anyway). Multiply that number by 20 thousand to give the odds of a spirit being present for the total number of counts needed for us to see it (7,812 trillion to one). If you take into account the number of seconds in a day or year, then the odds are extremely out of our favour.

That of course is based on the spirit being there in that second. However for that to happen the spirit will need to want to be at that point, as I will explain in a later chapter. This is not how I believe the spirit world works. Only a certain number of spirits can control where and what they are doing.

Another question that I would like to answer is regarding spirits who pass through walls. How can they do that? The answer is quite simple if you consider that spirits have access to the whole of time. At one point that wall did not or does not exist. As such the spirit can appear to walk through the wall. When in fact they are not. They are just drifting through the area when the wall doesn't exist.

So we can safely assume that the odds of seeing a spirit for a single frame is approximately 7,000 trillion to one, that is greater odds than winning the national or even international lottery.

That of course, is based only on the information I have covered above, however there is a lot more criteria that we haven't covered, which will greatly increase the odds. We will explain these as we work through this book.

As you work through this book, we will discuss one of two scenarios, one where spirits know they are dead and the second is when a spirit is not aware of its passing, so I want to ask a question, if a spirit is not aware its dead, what happens?

Well the answer is as simple as "The Sixth Sense" the movie staring Bruce Willis, when the film begins, he is not aware he is dead, as such he just continues doing what he would normally do on a normal day.

The same can be said for any spirit, if they are nurses for example, then they would just continue to work the ward, (for example those who claim nurses roam the hallways of abandoned hospitals etc.)

A spirit who is not aware of its passing, will just continue doing its daily tasks, or whatever it did in life, it will continue in death, "The Others" is another film that shows this in all its glory.

CHAPTER FOUR
The human body

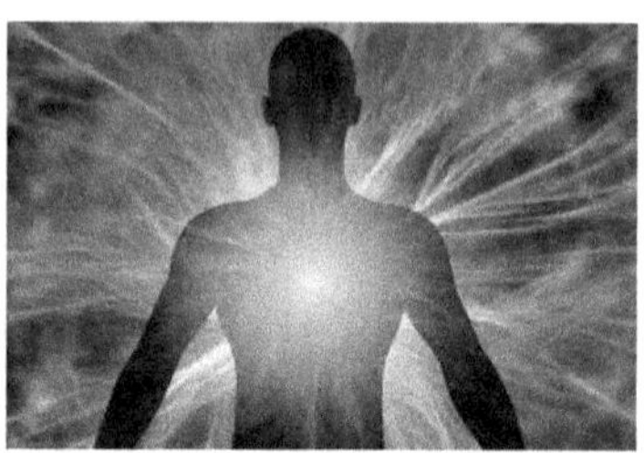

The human body is a very complicated machine. The question is, what does it have to do with the spirit world? Well it is my belief that the human body is a vessel for the spirit, and that is all. However unlike most of the body the brain is designed to complete additional tasks.

So I wish to discuss the human brain, and what it is used for. Scientists have already discussed what we use our brains for but in all cases, they cannot be 100% certain of the capacity of the human brain, so I have my own assumptions based on my theories and experience.

Firstly, you need to look into what spirits can actually do, they can communicate with each other, without the need for sound, (as sound requires air, and spirits do not have a physical body they cannot produce the air to create the sound. They can travel through time (4th dimension). They may do other things such as manipulate objects (telekinesis). So why as 3rd dimensional things, we cannot do it, if the body is just a vessel

I would like to suggest that you change your thought process and open your mind to the possibilities. The brain is two things, firstly it is the computer that the spirit uses to connect to the body, and secondly it is a prison.

What? A prison! What does it mean?

Let us imagine for a moment that you are a criminal. You have done something illegal and against the law. And you have been caught and sent to prison. (now I'm not saying that your spirit is a criminal, I'm just making a reference) What can you do? Well you cannot go out, you cannot speak to anyone who is not in the prison. You cannot do many of the things that you usually would as a 3rd dimensional being. Now what I want you to do is imagine that the prison is electronic. The whole prison is run through electronics, for example the doors, windows and gates and if the power goes out. Then everything opens and you are free to escape. You can get out as the doors no longer lock and hold you captive.

Now, I want you to imagine that your brain is a prison to the spirit. It is designed to stop the spirit doing certain things, for example telekinesis, telepathy and time travel. It is also designed to lock the spirit in to he body during the waking period. It is designed to keep things locked up and the only time those abilities are available is when we sleep. At which point our brains are shut down, much like the prison loosing its power. At this point we enter the dream realm, which I will discuss in detail in a later chapter.

As you can see from the paragraph above, it is very easy to imagine the brain as a form of prison cell for a spirit, and like a prison, good behaviour will lapse some of the restrictions you have been placed on your spirit. As such some individuals do have some special abilities. We have heard of people with telekinesis, psychic and other abilities. It is possible that these abilities have been made available due to some sort of good behaviour. maybe through the use of meditation, or possibly through the use of something else.

We also hear (especially with my father) that some people who suffer from illnesses such as dementia begin to speak with people who are not there. Is this a sign that those limitations that our brains have in place, are breaking down, and what these people are actually speaking to are other spirits.

Further to the information above, scientists have recently (2022) discovered that the brain actually functions throughout several different dimensions, the 3rd dimension only being a part of the complexity of the brain. They now claim that your brain actually traverses the 4th and 5th dimensions as well, based on the amount of information that our brains are capable of containing and the actual size of it, it is quite fees able that this information is correct. Our brains are uniquely complex organisms and we are only just beginning to understand some of it. There is still a long way to go before we can understand the complexities of that part of our body

Now, as we are discussing about the human body, I want to delve a little into disabilities, and I am aware that this section may cause some distress to some individuals, but, I wish to discuss this as it ties in with my principles above. As I have already stated, the human body is a vessel for a spirit, in much the same way that a glove is the vessel for a hand. We place hour hand inside the glove and use it to manipulate the glove.

However, let us imagine that for some reason we place two fingers into one finger hole in the glove. What we have now is a glove with four of the fingers working, and one finger not working. This is because we have not aligned our hand with the glove properly. Now let us take this idea and transfer it to the spirit and the human body. Let us say that the spirit does not for some reason align correctly with the human body, then do we have the same issue? Can the lack of voice be explained to the fact that the spirits voice box is not correctly connected to the bodies voice box, or if the spirits ears are not connected correctly to thee bodies ears. The question we need to ask is why would this happen?

The answer can be easily provided by knowing that not everything is made perfectly. We understand that several people have physical issues, which may cause problems. However is it possible that physical issues stop the spirit connecting correctly to that part of the body. We have DNA and modifications to that DNA, can also cause issues, can that also cause the spirit not to merge with the body correctly

The problem we have is that this idea cannot fully be proven at this moment in time. But I have identified with this because of my experiences. In my bedroom, several times during the night, whilst sleeping, upon waking I could not move, I could hear and speak to something I can only call a spirit. I assumed it was a spirit within me communicating with another spirit. I felt my spirit was not alighted with my body at the time.

I would like to delve into one more additional point about the human body, but firstly I need you to consider and think about a car or bus or anything like that, which we use as transport, and ask yourself, What does that item need to work?

In general the item whether it be car, plane, or train needs 4 separate items to run. Firstly we have the engine, the main system that makes the vehicle move, this is our brain, its the control unit for the entire body. The second thing that the vehicle needs is an operator, as time advances we are getting to the point where items wont need the operator but for now we do, as such I class this as the spirit. The item that connects to the engine in order to make the vehicle do as we require. The third item is the body itself, an engine and operator are no good if the vehicle has no body. This is the same with us, our body acts to hold everything together..

The final part of any vehicle is the fuel, without fuel the vehicle becomes useless, as such I believe that we creatures also have our own fuel cell, somewhat like a battery, I myself class that as the sole. And this is the object that passes from life to life. You can imagine that as we go through our life, we imprint our life onto that battery (sole) and as such that information can be passed onto the next in line.

However I do believe that our soles only have a set life span, just like a battery they only last so long. Lets say 80-100 years. When the battery dies the body dies along with it. Now the reason I say this is that we have online several stories of children who lived another life, in all circumstances that I have seen, the individual died in some form of accident, and not in old life. My assumption here is simple. Because the sole has an 80-100 year lifespan, it still has energy to spend if it is prematurely terminated, as such does that extra energy pass onto another child, allowing them to know about the passed live of the previous owner of that sole.

Its a concept I would love to know but as usual there is no evidence backing that up other than there must be some explanation as to how these children can remember their past lives. What I would love to know is how long these children actually live for, would their final age, and the age of the other person before the accidental death equal a total lifespan of 80-100 years. For example, if the original owner died at 35 would the child only live for around 45-65 years?

There is one more point I would like to question, and that is death. The question is quite a simple one, how long after death does our spirit actually detach from our body. We do not know if its instant or if its actually when the brain has finally broken down. Medical experts claim that even after death we still have some electrical signals in our brain. The biggest wonder here, is after we die, is our spirit still trapped inside the body (such like locked in syndrome) and if it is, then does the spirit still feel pain? For example, we are buried, or cremated. If our spirit is still locked into our body, do we feel or even see, what is happening, can we see our families saying goodbye, can we see the flames, or even feel the flames as they consume our bodies. A very scary thought to ponder.

CHAPTER FIVE
The dream world

We all dream, we get into bed, shut down our body and drift off in to the dream world. It is my belief that the dream world is just our spirits entering the fourth dimension (as our brains have shut down releasing the spirit). As anyone who remembers their dreams can tell you, we have no control over our dreams. We roam and dream, however I would like to introduce you to something else, an ability they call lucid dreaming.

Lucid dreaming is when an individual realises they are in a dream, and they then gain the ability as they are fully aware, to manipulate the dream anyway they want. As a lucid dreamer myself, I can go where I want, do what I want, and it is all in the dream world. I can also wake myself up if I wish to. This is not something that I can do all the time, but I have had several experiences of lucid dreaming throughout my life.

For a more easy explanation I would suggest watching "A nightmare on Elm Street 2" in this film, one of the teenagers, manages to control the dream and turn himself into a superhero to fight Freddy.

What you need to understand, that to be able to control your dreams you need to know your dreaming. Now. As I have already claimed we dream in the same realm that spirits live, then we can assume for a spirit to be able to control what they do, they have to know they are present into that world and they have to know they are dead.

Now I want to return to a previous point regarding the percentage chance of us seeing the spirit. We have already ascertained that the possibility is extremely low (1700 trillion to one), however, based on the details that the spirit would need to know they are dead in order to appear to us, reduces the percentage chance even more making it almost impossible for someone to see spirits every day (lets say there is a 50/50 change the spirit knows its dead, that would make 3400 trillion to one odds).

Have you ever dreamed of someone, and known who they are? I have, even though, I have never met that person before. I know who they are. What could be the explanation for this. My only assumption is that they are from a past life and with the ability to traverse time, they can appear to you or me in this life.

As an additional thought on dreams, scientists have made reports, that dreams we have last around 10 minutes. I have dreams of lifetimes, from a child through to an adult. My dreams can cover many years of life. I can clearly remember these dreams when waking. How can I explain it? As I have explained previously the answer is time.

Time is measured differently in the dream world. I have already stated that we have the ability in the third dimension to add up to at least 5 million in one second with innovative technology. So, let us take that as an example, and assume that the 4th dimensions works on that time frame. For every second we sleep we can assume that 5 million seconds has passed in the dream realm.

Let us do some maths. I know I hate maths too, but come on let us do some anyway.

Let us say that every second of sleep is equal to 5 million seconds in the dream realm.

That means that every minute wee sleep, in the dream world we have been there for 5 million minutes.

Now if we say we have been asleep for 10 minutes, we can add a 0 to that as such we have been there for 50 million minutes

now if we transfer that into real life and say that we have been around for 50 million minutes, then we can state with ease that we have been there for the equivalent of 190 years in their time frame (more than a full lifetime)

as such it is possible that in 10 minutes of sleep, we can live an entire life in the 4th dimension. This adds to the idea of seeing spirits. If you think that in 10 minutes a spirit could have lived for 190 years, then the chances of actually seeing one becomes even more unlikely

I would like to take a minute or two to discuss the different types of dreams. From my experiences there are two different dreams that an individual can have, one is what I would call a normal dream, and the other is a dream that has spiritual meaning.

A normal dream is quite simply explained as having no feelings. What do I mean by this? To put it simply, no matter what you dream about you do not have any feelings, or a sense of sadness, happiness, joy or fear. These do not exist in the normal dream realm. Yes, once you wake up you can have these feelings about the dream, however whilst dreaming you do not feel anything.

The second type of dream is the spiritual dream. This type of dream is given to you for one reason or another, generally to send you a message. As I discussed earlier, my old dog Paige visited me in a dream to say goodbye. It was a spiritual dream and the experience left me bursting with complex feelings.

To explain, take the dream of my dog visiting me, whilst my dog was in the dream, I felt fear, but not fear as in danger, or fright, it was the type of fear you might feel if you saw a skeleton climb out of the ground in front of you. For some reason in that dream I knew that it was a dead dog that was visiting me, although I did not realise what it was until the following morning, the feeling was strong and was present all through the dream.. it is generally these dreams that cause individuals to wake up screaming, for example a nightmare.

So in general a spiritual dream has feelings where as a normal dream feels like watching a TV show. I regularly and frequently experience dreams from the spirit world.

I would like for a moment delve into religions, such as Christianity and the Muslim religion. It may seem a little strange discussing this within this section regarding dreams, however please bear with me.

According to the muslin religion, Mohammed flew to heaven on a winged horse. Now our own logic thought, and of course evidence proves that this is not possible, as there is no such thing as a winged horse. However there is such a thing as a spiritual dream. A dream that can feel real and seems so real to the individual, they believe it to be real. I am not saying that the story is false. What I am trying to say is that the explanation can be as easy as Mohammed possibly having a spiritual dream.

The same can be said regarding Mary and the angel, who visited her to inform her of her pregnancy. Again, this could have been a spiritual dream, it just feels real to the individuals, who may not experience this type of dream normally.

Whilst we are currently discussing the dream world. I would like to cover one more subject that i think may be pertinent to this topic and that is coma patients. I would like to make it clear that the following comments are based on my thoughts and there is no evidence to support my conjecture.

As we have already discussed, the human body is a machine, and the spirit is the controller of that machine. Like all machines, it can run on its own, without the aid of a spirit. There are automatic things that the body does to keep itself active, such as breathing. How else would the body survive during the night when we are asleep if we did not breath? An example is a car engine running without a driver or passenger in the car.

My theory revolves around the principle that a coma patient is someone whose spirit for some reason cannot return to the body. And as such the spirit is stuck in the dream world. The reasons for this could be wide and varied, but we know that it happens.

As we all know coma patients can come out of a coma or even die. So how can we explain this outcome, and how can we explain the time frame that some coma patients can spend years in that comatose state.

Well, we can use the information we have already read. The fact that the spirit is stuck in the spirit world. It would need to know that it is there, but it also needs to return to the body and of course there are two options open to it.

Option one is that the spirit realises its in a dream, or dreaming, at which point as I explained it can wake itself up. The second options is that the spirit believes that it is dead. As such, can this misunderstanding terminate the connection between the mind and the spirit and thus ending the body's life.

Some of us may be aware of the rumours that if your spirit falls in a dream and hits the floor, the result is that the individual can die. Does that mean if the spirit believes its dead, the body will automatically terminate itself or to be specific and to the point, does the spirit disconnect itself from the brain, and if so, does the brain then shut down the body causing death.

This may explain how coma patients can either wake up or pass over. As I have already stated, this is theory cannot be proven however it is feasible based on what we have already discussed.

CHAPTER SIX
spiritualists and mediums

Firstly let me make this perfectly clear, I am going into details and information in this chapter that will make it sound like spiritualists and mediums are fake, however I want to explain in this chapter is based on my own personal experiences and as such does not conform to all who claim to be able to speak with spirits.

My own experiences tell me that most spiritualists or mediums are in fact not speaking to spirits but are instead actually using a psychic ability to let us say read your mind. Let me explain why

Firstly, I have spoken to a spirit, in full conversation, in the middle of the night, I asked the spirits name and was given the answer in full. I cannot for the life of me remember the last name, but I was given both the first and last names.

I want to point out that I had to ask the spirit for the information. I tried using only my thoughts, but it did not work, and the spirit did not respond. When I eventually asked the question out loud, I heard a voice as if there was a little girl in my bedroom. Let me explain what happened.

It was 2017, I had gone to bed and gone to sleep. I was awoken early in the morning with a feeling of not being alone. It was hard to explain the feeling, but it is what happens whenever there is a spirit about. I found I could not move, and even thought I tried I could not speak, I was paralysed in my bed.

I forced myself to cough and it took a while, but at that moment I once again had control over my voice box, although when I spoke it sounded extremely slow, and deep, not the normal sound my voice makes. Even thought I could not move my body or limbs, my eyes were open and I was starring at my wall. But there was something in the room, I could sense it. It was at that point I asked the question "Who is there?"

Immediately a voice, a small girl voice replied "Emma". I responded once again with "Emma who?" she replied with her last name, although at present I cannot remember what that was. I then continued with the questions and asked "what are you doing here?" to which she replied "my mammy killed me and buried me in the back under the arch". I then asked how old she was and she replied "5" finally I asked here when she died and she replied "1904". IT was at this point I appeared to have fallen back to sleep.

Please note that at the time we lived in a terraced house with a yard and not a garden. So, at this moment I realised that this little girl was not from my current location. But had travelled to this house where I was living.

Now I want to point out that we knew there was spiritual activity in the house, however myself and my family assumed there was only one spirit. It turns out there were at least three. I have had contact with each of them in one way or another.

I never actually spoke to the little girl again, thought approximately one week later, I woke up in the same state to find myself pinned to the bed. I felt something on top of me, it took me a moment and some effort to force my arm to move. I managed to grab at the arm of whatever it was pinning me to the bed, at which point I saw an arm and started to manifest itself before whoever or whatever it was laughed and disappeared. The laugh was that of a male figure, but other than that, I cannot give any further information.

On another evening whilst I slept, I was awoken by another presence who turned out to be my Nana, who passed over back in 2007. before I could say anything, she informed me that my father would be joining her shortly. Within two months my father passed over due to a long term illness with his brain.

On a separate occasion, I was visited by Paige, an English bull terrier that I took care of for nearly four years, her owners requested that I took care of her when they were absent. She visited me during the night and the following morning I got a phone call to inform me that she had died

during the night. We discovered later that it was due to some sort of cancer.

As you can see, I have experienced several occasions where I have deal with spirits. So why do I say what I do regarding mediums and spiritualists? Well the answer is simple. If they are communicating with spirits themselves, they would be able to tell you who it is they are speaking to. I managed to get the name from the spirit, so whey do they fail in this task.

An additional point I want to make, is that in most cases, spiritualists and mediums use vague information. Such as he was a gardener. Or he suffered in his last few days. However, if they were speaking with spirits, they should be able to be more specific. They would be able to tell you exactly the information you want to know. How they specifically died, and their names. For example, I have already demonstrated above that this information can be asked and obtained quite easily.

In my experience listening to mediums, there has only been one that truly impressed me out of the hundreds I have seen, and I still have my doubts. As the individual she chose to pass messages onto, had never been to our church before and never came again, even thought he claimed to now be a strong believer (this made me question the validity of her mediumship.) other mediums have given me reason not to believe that they can communicate with spirits. As I have already stated, the reason is because the information they pass over to you, for example;

This person had a real nice garden – how many people do you know that have a really nice garden?
The person suffered before they died – How many people do you know suffered before they died?
The person used profane language – again this is most of the people I know.

As I have previously explained, the details provided by most mediums can be to simple and easy to associate with more than half of the people that you know or knew. As such, it makes me wonder if they are actually able to communicate with spirits or as I have already explained just using some sort of mind reading technique.

For this reason, I believe that most mediums and spiritualists are not actually speaking with the spirits but have tuned their minds to be able to read minds in a way, but only to point where they can see images or ideas. If you carefully observe a medium working, they will pick on someone specific. This may be because, as I believe they are reading them. The individuals chosen possible has a mind that I like to call open and easy to read, and as such they are chosen because the medium is obtaining images from them.

At the same time, if you take a private reading from a medium, and they cannot read from you, they will tell you something along the lines, you are not open to a reading, meaning they cannot read you. Why would a medium tell you that if they were in fact speaking with spirits? I have experienced this myself, a friend of the family arranged a medium to come and give the family reading, I was working at the time, so couldn't go, however at the last moment my shift was changed, and I ended up attending, to be told that they couldn't read from me. Which honestly in turn made me think they too were fake, and that our friend had actually some deal in place with her, and had given her the information that my family wanted to hear.

I state this for two reasons, firstly in a previous chapter. I explained that a spirit must know its dead to be able to reach our realm, and the change that a newly dead relative would know they are dead is very slim, as such if this is actually the case, a newly dead relatives would generally not be able to return to the 3rd dimensional

Secondly as I have already explained. I have spoken with spirits, to be able to communicate with them I need to speak. I cannot use my mind as mediums claim to. To give you an actual understanding imagine being in a room with someone, and just talking with them, and listening to them, that is how it is with spirits, its not in the mind, you can actually hear them like you can hear your friend.

So it is my belief, that mediums and spiritualists, are using psychic abilities rather than actually dealing with spirits, and those abilities are enabling the medium to connect to the recipients mind to obtain images, rather than dealing with spirits.

Don't get me wrong I am not saying that spiritualists and mediums are frauds, I'm just saying that they are not exactly what they appear to be, in my opinion.

CHAPTER SEVEN
Spirits and time

I have already explained that I believe the 4th dimension is time, and as such spirits have the full access to time, however I need to make a point that I do not believe that spirits have control of all time.

Let me explain, what I mean, since the 4th dimension is as we have already discussed "time", space is not part of it (I believe space to be the 5th dimension) as such a spirit cannot occupy the same space as itself, and since your spirit is in your body, your spirit cannot visit you. By that I mean, that your spirit is already present at the moment inside you. And because of that your spirit when you die, cannot come back to this moment and visit you because your spirit is already here. You yourself cannot be in the same place at the same time as yourself. (unless you have an identical twin, even then its not you)

That results in the principle that a spirit can only access time frames, that do not currently exist within your life, meaning in practice that they can only travel the time frame after you die, and the time frame before you lived.

However I wish to narrow that down even more by stating that before you were born your spirit never exist. So it cannot travel into a period that does not exist. There is more chance that the spirit that resides in your body at this moment was created from your life. It is possible that the sole, (as we have already discussed) has been passed from person to person, but I believe the spirit is created from the life you live.

Have you ever heard of anyone say, they have seen their own spirit? Or a family member say I saw you before you were born? I have not.

this can also be proven through two different avenues.

Firstly a quick look on You Tube will provide you with examples of children who can remember their past lives, and have been proven to be correct in their descriptions of their previous lives. As explained previously, this could be due to the sole being shared.

And secondly using meditation you can sees past lives. There are people who will help you do this, although most of what I hear, I do not believe. You will find that in almost all cases, the individual was some one special. I have heard of someone who was on the famous ship titanic, someone who was the leader of an army, or at least the leader of military, however in most cases, people would have been normal common folk. Like you and me.

So what does this mean? Well it is quite simple. I believe that spirits do have access to all of time from the moment you die, until your spirit is passed on to another dimension.

Let us say for arguments sake, you died tomorrow. Your spirit would be free, and could travel through time whenever and wherever it wanted, up until it was sent to another dimension, let us say 1000 of our years (5000 million spirit years). The principle that your spirit could travel through 1000 years, easily going where it wants back and fourth as it wishes.

Now if you aware you are dead, then you would be able to control where and what you wanted to do in the 4th dimension much like with lucid dreaming. So you could visit family at their homes. Some people can do this whilst asleep, and its generally called an out of body experience, some people can do this at will, where others have more difficulties.

Based on the above we can now examine the idea of time travel. Is it possible? And the simple answer is yes and no. in our physical bodies time travel is not possible, as we cannot manipulate time itself, however within the 4th dimension we can travel to when or where we want. As such travel into the future is possible. So we need to ask ourselves, is this how people who claim to have been in the future, or people who have predicted the future managed to do it? Was it in their dream state that they visited the future? Was the new york trade towers destruction in 2011 seen in a dream by someone (Nostradamus) before the tragedy

occurred? And if so it may result in the fact that the individual may have had the ability to lucid dream.

CHAPTER EIGHT
My history

I want to take a chapter to explain my entire life, and experiences for you to understand where my principles and ideas come from. Ever since I was young baby I have had to deal with the paranormal, spirits and strange occurrences which I cannot explain.

It all started, as with most stories, from the day I was born. My father was a military soldier in the British army based in lipstadt, Germany, and I was in a British military hospital in a place called Iserlohn. At the time we lived in a small flat which was allocated by the army to my father, for the first 8 months of my life we had a spirit in the flat, who my parents dubbed "Herman the German" I will call him Herman for short.

My mother always claimed that Herman was a second spirit that was fighting with the spirit in me, to take control, and just to rub salt in the would, that the wrong spirit won. (my family are a lot of fun, it was not meant as an insult rather a laugh)

Herman, it was assumed was there for me, as most of the things that happened all related to me, for example my nappies would be lined up ready for use, my plate and baby bottles and food would be laid out on the workbench in the kitchen ready for use. My parents had not done these tasks. Many other small, unexplained things would happen that were associated with me.

On one occasion, whilst we were attending a party, Herman had turned on all the water taps in the house and filled the bath and sinks resulting in a flood of the property (Sound familiar)

These things only ever happened whilst my mother was at home, since my father was always on duty away from the flat, he didn't really believe in the paranormal and would just write it off to my mother missing her family.

The final straw happened on the 27 December 1976, I was 6 months old and my mother had had a really bad day with me. It was my mother and fathers wedding anniversary and they were celebrating with a meal that had been prepared by my father. I had been restless all day and crying. My mother finally put me in my cot in the bedroom hoping that I would settle. All the time I was screaming.

However the moment my mother and father picked up their cutlery to eat, I stopped crying. They ate the meal, and as soon as they had finished eating, I started crying again. When my mother entered my bedroom, she was shocked to discover that the furniture in the room had been moved around, my cot and cupboard had completely swapped places. It was at that time my father finally realised something was in the flat.

They ended up visiting churches, and asking priests for help, which was where the idea came from for the second spirit fighting to control me.

It was shortly after that my family came back to the UK for a holiday and when we returned to Germany, Herman was no longer in the flat. Or at least we suffered no more paranormal activity. That was the first of many interactions and experiences with spirits, me and my family would have to deal with.

During the first seven years of life, my parents have told me that I used to have an imaginary friend, who I used to spend a lot of time playing and talking to but based on my experiences growing up and taking into account all of the interactions, I can not remember an imaginary friend. I must ask myself was this actually an imaginary friend or actually a spirit. Who spent time with me, and if so was it actually the spirit we had dubbed as Herman. (This is something I must ask children who have imaginary friends, or ask questions as to who they are talking to)

My next visit was at the age of 10 years, whilst working on a paper round, I heard a voice at around 5 o clock in the morning from a young girl calling out my name. The name calling caught my attention and in turn I lost concentration causing an accident. I had turned my head to see where the voice came from. I rode my bike into a car, and the incident ended up with me in hospital having stitches in my head.

Until the age of 16 I had several nights of interrupted sleep and in a lot of cases felt scared but the feelings that accompanied the waking moments. Today I understand what that feeling I had means, but in the earlier days I did not have any understanding of what it was that was happening to me.

I remember one dream imp-articular. I was laid in bed, I thought I was awake, and I could sense something horrible climbing the stairs in my house, I don't know how to explain it, but I could feel a horrible presence and it was getting closer, I tried to wake myself up to find myself in exactly the same situation. This went on about 4 or five times, I would think I was awake and the feeling would return, eventually I managed to actually wake up, and could not get back to sleep. I couldn't move, or speak or scream.

From the age of 16 I have experienced many different spiritual events. Starting with voices from nowhere. Visions of figures that have not been there and speaking with children who cannot possibly speak. Also speaking to spirits, whilst in bed on an evening. As well as having spirits approach me to say goodbye. All these evens are covered in this book.

At present I still have spirits talk to me on regular intervals, including as I explained earlier, my Nana telling me that my father was about to die. Most of my history can be explained through the simple fact that I have some sort of connection with the spirit world. Which allows me to communicate with them. That is the only possible explanation I can think of that covers what I have experienced in my lifetime.

My whole life has involved spirits, in one way or another. I have many other abilities which I cannot explain. For example I often did leaflet deliveries with my grandfather and I was able to take the exact numbers of leaflets needed to complete the task without counting them.

Many have done experiments on the ability to know when someone or something is calling you by name. I have this ability also, although not all the time. Just occasionally. There are many other abilities that have manifested themselves within me, such as the ability to know if someone is good or bad, or the ability to know if someone has a mental health issue just from looking at them. I also have the uncanny ability to know if someone is faking something towards me, such as mediumship or bluffing in poker. To this date I have not lost money in a poker tournament, and I have played many poker games regularly finishing in the last 10 players. Often in the last five players with several wins in my pocket. The only problem I have is that I get bored with the game. If it were not for the boredom, I could probably make a living from playing poker professionally.

As a final thought for this chapter, I do want to point out, that I have seen what I associate as the figure for death, or the manifestation of what I believe was death. It happened about two days after I grabbed a spirit pinning me to the bed. Again, I was woken during the night, however this time, I was not looking into the room, I was looking at the room as

though it was not there. It was as if for that moment, I could see through time, the walls of the room were there, but they were translucent, as if the images were ghostly.

Beyond the wall I could see a figure dressed in black, matching the description we know of as death, in his black cloak with a scythe. Stood next to him was a figure of a wolf style creature in a man's body, now what or who that was I have no clue.

Unfortunately, although I tried, I could not clear my throat and could not cough, nor could I speak or move. Otherwise I would have spoken and asked questions. However it was after this that my dogs, Wiebke and Paige (two of my dogs who have passed over) arrived and would sleep at the end of my bed every night. I could physically feel them between my legs, and that was where they sleep when alive. On one occasion the spirit of Wiebke even barked when I moved my foot during the night. I can only assume that it was my spirit that moved and she was warning me or my spirit not to.

Whilst they were in my bed I was not bothered by any spirits visiting me, except for one night. I woke up with that feeling of not being alone. I was facing the wall in my bedroom, but this time I could not speak at all even though it tried. I never found out who was in my room that night. A shame really as I have a feeling that it was actually my grandmother who had died in the house only a few months earlier although I could have been either Emma the little girl or the male figure that pinned me to the bed.

Here is a simple but interesting question for you to contemplate. We have all heard of the words deja vu, and what it means. For those that do not, its basically means that we have been in and done whatever it is that we are witnessing before. The questions simply asks. If our spirit can traverse the spirit realm, is deja vu the result of us having travelled into the future in our dreams and actually appearing at that specific moment and witnessing what is going on? And as such have, we already been there and done that, causing this feeling of repetition.

CHAPTER NINE
Disabilities and spirits

So, I have covered in an earlier chapter about spirits aligning to the body. I want to cover this in a little more detail sin this chapter.

I explained about how we need to put our hand in a glove correctly in order to use all the fingers in that glove. If we do not align our hands as they need to be, then we cannot possibly control all aspects of the glove.

I believe this may work in the same way with spirits and the human body. If for some reason the spirit cannot align correctly with the body, then we end up with not being able to use the part of the body. So, if for example they cannot alight with the body correctly we end up with something like "locked in syndrome". This basically means that you cannot move any part of the body at all, nor talk. There is a story online of one guy who experienced this. It is an interesting tale, and explains how he could see, hear and feel bug could not move. Much like the situation I was in when I was awoken and spoke to the little girl in my bedroom.

It for example, as already explained we have issues with our DNA (deoxyribonucleic acid) this can cause malfunctions in the alignment. If you think of a glove being created with a malfunction in which, for example the fifth finger is blocked off. So you cannot insert your finger, then again we would not be able to use that finger. Take into consideration that an individual whose voice box is the problem, they would not be able to speak, or for instance someone whose ears are the problem, the spirit would not be able to hear.

We can also associate this with any other disability, if you assume my ideas are correctly

I would like to discuss disabilities now, such as multiple personality disorder, or psychosis. In all circumstances these are basically the thoughts, words of many different people all interacting at the same time. In the example of MPD (multiple personality disorder) we can have an individuals with many different personalities.

If you accept my ideas, the possibility of those personalities are spirits that inhabit one body or person. Something in the DNA has resulted in the body being the host for several spirits rather than just one.

It is generally believed that MPD is caused when trauma causes the individual to block out what is happening to them. Or as I have explained already, the spirit leaves the body and enters into the dream realm so that they don't have to endure the torture that they are being witness to. Currently the body is free. Is it possible that a second, third or more spirits are entering the body, and when the original spirit returns you end up with two or more separate spirits living within one body.

We also hear of people who are schizophrenic. These people claim to hear voices telling them to act out, sometimes dangerously, again I have to ask if these voices are actually spirits? As with the real world we live in there are spirits that act negatively, and positively as sometimes real people do. Could these spirits actually be interacting with these people

It is all interesting to contemplate when you sit down and thing about the possibilities. But the issue with it all is proving it. unfortunately at this present moment in time, there is now way to prove this information, however there are ways to test it. And one of my aims is to try and achieve that.

Examining any disability, we can identify a situation that matches my theories above, regarding spiritual alignment.

CHAPTER TEN
communication with spirts

I have already explained about talking to individuals who I could not possibly have spoken to spirits, as well as hearing voices in previous chapters in this book. So I want to discuss the possibilities of communication. And the main question I want to answer but probably will not able to without more evidence. Is am I communicating through some sort of telepathy.

Let me ask you a question, what will happen if you jump of a building? Well from knowledge of gravity and previous experiences. We know that if we jump of a building we will fall downwards. We do not have to physically jump of a building to know that. The idea is imprinted in our heads, as such, we cannot assume anything else other than falling, for example we cannot believe that someone jumping off a building would float up rather than fall and as such because of our beliefs we would not jump off a building without protection (a parachute)

The same principle can be said with regards to speech. As we all know for someone to talk to us, they must move their mouth in a certain way. So we look at their mouth as they talk. Those who are not looking at us we assume they are talking. as there mouths are working.

As such our brains are programmed to know that if the mouth is not moving we cannot possibly be speaking, so if we know for example that a child cannot speak then we cannot possibly hear them speak. Our brain is attuned to that. As such. It would be impossible to hear them through telepathy.

As I explained earlier, we can look at a ventriloquist and realise that if the mouth is not moving but the mouth of the dummy is, then we associate the voice with the dummy, and to our brains it looks like the dummy is speaking. Although we know different. Our brain generates that vision to us. Our brains are programmed to associate mouth movement with sound.

Now is it possible that if we do not actually see the mouth of an individuals, we can really communicate with the brain directly. We call this telepathy. I can only assume yes due to my previous experience or if we are not aware that a child or individual cannot speak, can we still hear them?

In all circumstances where I have communicated with what I believe to be a spirit, I have not seen the mouth, but have clearly hear the voice. Again with regards to the bed and the little girl, I couldn't move or speak and after a bit of force from myself I was able to speak. Was that me speaking telepathy? I do not know, but I believe it was a possibility, as I have already stated, the voice I used was not that of my own, it was slow, deep and rough.

As such, if this is actually true, am I able to speak through telepathy as long as I am not looking at the individual and as long as I am not aware of any speech problems, then can I do that with all individuals. Can I speak to children and or adults who cannot speak. I have not had the chance to prove that as a fact, and as such am unable to speculate on the situation. I understand that I would have to retrain my brain so that it does not associate movement with speech.

I have also pointed out that to speak with the girl in the bedroom, I had to physically speak. Just thinking about the questions was not good enough and did not result in the answer I sought. This means that most mediums cannot possibly be speaking with spirits. As I have already stated, we need to speak to communicate, and most just stand thinking.

As an additional thought based on my principles of our programmed brain, can a baby really communicate through telepathy? We cannot of course hear it as we are programmed to know that a new born baby cannot speak. Nevertheless, a baby is not programmed, as such can they truly communicate through telepathy.

For a moment I want you to think about the last question. If it is possible then a baby already knows our language, as such does that come from a previous life. If the answer is yes, then does a new born baby remember its past life. If previous lives exist? There are a lot of questions that we could answer if my theories are correct.

I want to delve a little into what I believe with regards to spirits and communication, (being able to hear). We are all aware, and have heard stories of children and animals having the ability to know, hear or even see spirits, so what you may ask yourself is the difference between us and them.

We all know that dogs can hear at a higher frequency than we can. As such I have to ask do spirits speak at a higher frequency, for this I am looking at the possibility of some sort of ultra sonic recording device, that will allow me to record all sound above our hearing range. Children have also been tested and those tests have relieved that even children can hear at a slightly higher frequency than adults are capable of. As such I am looking at purchasing a good quality ultra sonic microphone, and software to process the incoming data in a hopes that we can catch some sounds.

Going back a little to the section in this book about time and our perceiving of vision. (the human boy can see 100-200) frames of information per second, it is fees able that animals have a capacity to see more frames.

I want to you think of something for a moment, we as living creatures are a lot like a computer, we have a set frequency that we work at. Based on our five senses, let us say, as well as other things such as feeling pain, we need to be able to process all this information as quickly as possible. Let us say that we as humans work at 5khz per second, that means that our brain can do 5000 things per second (or 5000 ticks). Taking into account, our vision, being 200 frames per second, our hearing, and such, each thing would have to have its own section of that 5000 ticks. Now, what I want to ask is the following, a dog for example lives a lot less than we do, the equivalent is 7 years to every one years of ours. Does this mean that a dogs brain works 7 times faster than ours, if so, that would in turn mean that a dog would run at around 35khz per second, resulting in over 1400 frames per second in vision. We all know that dogs have better vision and hearing than humans. Could this be why dogs and other animals actually sense spirits better than us, can them 1400 frames per second make a massive difference?

Also research tells us that dogs cannot see two dimensional objects such as TV, although I don't believe that, could it be that because a dog can see at say 1400 frames per second, that that TV, just looks to a dog like still images, if you take into consideration that we see 60 TV images a second, to a dog, each image would last 20 times longer. Imagine if your TV showed you only 3 images a second.

Now, a quick one, take a look at an insect, a fly, wasp or anything like that, they have multiple eyes, why? If you believe in evolution then you know as well as I do that our bodies are designed for a reason, so what's the reason, well here is something to think about. We will look at a wasp, average lifespan about 8 weeks. That means that we as humans last about 800 times longer than a wasp. In retrospect that would mean that a wasps mind runs at a whopping 800 times faster than ours. Meaning in excess of

4Ghz speed. Now, that would equal 160,000 images a second. Is the reason they are provided with so many eyes, so that the eyes can actually pick up all these images. Are the eyes set up so that each one takes a photo, it is known online that wasps can have between 1000, and 16000 different lenses, that would mean each eye could pick up photos, just 100 frames per second for 1600 eyes.

To test this theory and to try to catch spirits, I am looking at purchasing a super high speed camera, there is one on the market that can take up to 1 million images a second, I believe this would be a great investment for this, however the price is astronomical with just a normal 2000 images per second camera coming in at a cool £10,000.

CHAPTER ELEVEN
Meditation

I want to take some time to discuss meditation, what it is and how does it help when we talk about spirits and communication.

Meditation is a way that we as human beings of the 3rd dimension can clear our minds and relax our thoughts. In a way it is how we can attain our innocence. When we meditate, we essentially leave all our worldly issues back in the real world and enter what can be described as a fantasy world. It could possibly be classed as the dream world or the 4th dimension. Only we know we are there and as such have control.

If you accomplish mediation properly your body can enter a state of paralysis, whilst you are meditating. Much like that as described earlier with regards to the bed. A true deep mediation will enable this to happen, and is why, under no circumstances should you attempt to meditate without prior knowledge on what you are doing, or without the assistance of someone who knows what they are doing. One may not be able to return to their own bodies if this go array.

A good meditation will allow your spirit to enter the 4th dimension, as I have explained above, and allow your body to relax some of the constraints that are associated with the human body. Which in turn is why mediums meditate regularly.

Using mediation, we can also visit different locations, for example there have been documented stories of individuals who have visited someone and were able to detail what for instances, was on the table in an individuals home.

I meditate regularly. I have round that if I do not mediate then my abilities somewhat lapse. And it is much more difficult for me to connect with the spirit world. So a daily routine lasting around 30-40 minutes suffices. I will sit on my own in a quiet room, place soothing composition on the computer, normally forest noises and begin a self meditation where I will visit a special garden that I have created in my dream state. There I will sit relax and let my real life fade away into he distance, this allows my mind to fully relax. When in the state of meditation, one can also receive visitors, messages or gifts from people who are deceased or even alive.

Most mediums will inform you that you have a spirit guide. I do not believe this to be true. If you listen to most mediums, nearly all of them have one thing in common. There spirit guide is an American Indian or even a nun, however there are millions of spirits in the world. So how is it that most mediums have the same type of spirit guide? What I believe is that the spirit guide is what mediums use to explain where they get the informations that they pass onto the client. Yet I have already explained how they do that, i do not believe it has anything to do with spirits, but more to do with the ability to read mind or at least in some way shape or form read minds.

Mediation allows us to clear our thoughts, it allows us to remove any bad or unkempt baggage. Shall we say from our minds. As one of the most important aspects of communication with spirit world is that we have to be innocent.

At the end of every one of my meditations and before I leave my garden there is an area where I stand and have a shower. The water that drops down from above is silver and as it flows over my body it turns black and runs down the drain. This is me washing away all the bad feelings in my mind and body. As time goes on the water begins to turn slowly back to the original colour. Which in turn means that the bad and negative has been washed out of me.

It is documented all over the internet that children can regularly see spirits, but adult cannot. This reason they have associated that with, is the innocents of the child. A child has not had its brain programmed to know that spirits cannot be seen or heard. Like most of us have been conditioned to believe. As such a child is innocent. By meditating we can, after a while, get back to the state where although we still believe that spirits are not real, we start to break down the walls within our minds that stop us from seeing and hearing what is all around us

Once you have started to break down the walls between our world and the spirit world, you then start to truly believe in spirits. These two things together then allow you to work in the world of spirits.

I suppose the easiest way to explain it is to look at the film the "Matrix". At the beginning of the film Neo believes all the rules of the earth. He only knows what he experiences. He believes what his mind is telling him. It takes a while for him to learn the real rules of the earth. He acquires the knowledge that the earth is operated through a computer program. Once he understand and becomes aware of the new word, he beings to realise that he can do many things that a normal human would not be able to do, for example suddenly he can slow down time and fight at incredible speeds.

All the above is imaginary and in a film, but what if there was in fact some truth to the issue. What we need to break down is the wall that we have created in our brains. This is stopping most people from communication with the 4th dimension. Mediated allows us to slowly break down that barrier.

I want to discuss ghost hunts and explain what they are. A ghost hunt is basically a gathering of people at a location that previously claims to have a ghost or spiritual activity. They spend an evening trying to obtain evidence of spirits within any building or location. In almost all cases they are a group of individuals usually consisting of a couple of mediums, a technical person and possibly another who arranges the gatherings.

Now although I enjoy going on these ghost hunts, I really hate the way that these groups play on peoples minds. I have witnessed it on several occasions. I have already explained how I have the ability to read when people are Faking it, shall we say and in most cases, it is false

The best and simplest way is where, at an event, it can be faked, is with the table tipping method. This involves a small table that is very unsteady on the floor, and everyone attending places a hand on the table and miraculously the table begins to move. However those of us who are are can clearly see that someone is leading the movements. There movements are just that little bit quicker than everyone else that is attending can see. Sadly they stand out a mile when I observe them and relate to the falseness (possibly due to the Autistic traits). It ruins the night for the participating, so I do not take part in these events any more.

A second easily manipulated result comes in the form of the glass on the table. Again same principle. Everyone places a finger on the glass and the glass appears to move. Once more watching intently, you can clearly see who is moving the glass.

I am also aware of what some people class as possession. Alas, experience tells me that a spirit cannot enter a body that already contains a spirit (this is why I wake up when a spirit is near my body). As such it is impossible for a possession to take place in the manner that these groups portray. To tell you the truth, I have yet to find an actual group that does not manipulate the results of a ghost hunt, but when I do, that will be the main group that I will use for my experiments.

I want to make it clear, that in my opinion, most groups are although they claim not to be, doing what they do for entertainment purposes, and not for the actual evidential reasons, that I wish to pursue.

I would like to show you an image. That was taken during one of my many ghost hunts. In this situation we were in a laser quest building that had been built over the top of an old prison where the prisoners were executed. Before the actual ghost hunt took place, I walked around the location and took several photographs, whenever I felt the presence of a spirit. I would take a photo capture. Please note this image has been enlarged digitally compared to the actual photo. The actual part of the image was only a few millimetres in height.

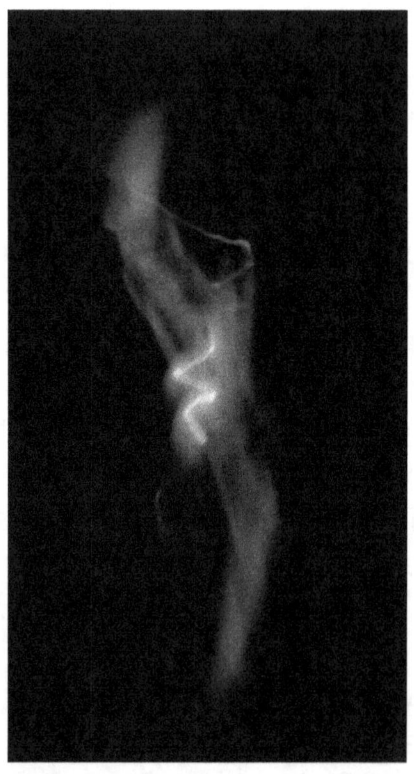

I have spent many a day studying this image in an attempt to ascertain what it is we are actually seeing. I can honestly say, I have come up with two possibilities. The first is that this is the manifestation of a full body, the head being at the top jutting forward then the legs being at the bottom of the body.

My second thought was that this was the image of a limb, like that of a leg. An example is that it is only a section of the spirit much like an x ray. However, I will point out that I also investigated the site a second time to ensure there was nothing that could have possibly caused that bolt in the middle of the picture.

Could the bolt be an actual spirit? Who knows? I know that this was a very unique photograph, which I was extremely pleased about.

I would like to take this moment to discus the equipment used in ghost hunts, and why I believe that the equipment is actually useless.

Firstly spirit boxes. This is a device that is supposed to connect to the essence of a spirit allowing them to communicate with the living, however the fact of the matter is that spirit boxes are just broken radios, let me explain

a spirit box is a device that is designed to skip through all the radio channels one after another in a series of seconds. It may pass through two or three radio channels in one second. This is why we hear constant rhythm of music, silence, static, silence, static, silence, music etc.

the static part is the actually radio channel the silence it it tuning in.

now let us assume that heart FM is playing a song and they announcing it on the radio. Let us say the host is saying "that was Eminem with superman, and now we have dance monkey"

So we have our spirit box on, and I decide to ask it "who are you" suddenly the spirit box tunes into heart FM and we hear EM (part of Eminem) we instantly assume we are talking to Em, or Emma. So I give it a moment and ask "What do you do" the spirit box goes through all its channels and picks up heart again, once again this time we hear "dance" (from dance monkey) well now we have a girl called Emma who loves to dance.

it is too easy to manipulate people when they really have their hearts set on something, and as I said this device is one of the useless devices used

EMF readers are the second item I wish to discuss. These devices pick up electro magnetic fields, now what everyone needs to be aware of is that everything electronic gives off an electromagnetic field even the device itself. Even your own body gives of a small electromagnetic field. If there are any electronic systems where you are using these devices they can be set off. If someone is using their phone or switching there phones on in their pockets, these devices will go off, even your watch can set one off. Be ware when using these devices.

I want to point out that the other day we were doing an investigation, and I was stood over the other side of the large hall, and used the radio, The EMF meter which was sat at the opposite end of the hall started flashing. The closer I got with the radio, the more it flashed. So even from around 40 foot away I was effecting the EMF reader. Imagine what a host who has a phone can do just a few feet away.

Ouija boards are another item that attracts a lot of bad press. Now I want to make clear I don't use them. I don't tempt fate and I would suggest they are never used. You don't need to use one to contact spirits as I have already explained. However again based on the comment above its just a glass on a board. Watching you will see someone moving the glass, if a spirit really wanted to contact you they would move the glass themselves, the glass does not need to be touched.

A final item I wish to talk about is orbs. Many people assume an orb is a spirit, however it is more fees-able that an orb is just a speck of dust or an insect that is way to close to the lens of the camera, yes some orbs can move around, however the slightest breeze can cause that. Even a breeze that you cannot feel. I believe that 99% of cases where people see orbs, its actually just dust practicals.

#

So after writing this book, I have to ask myself what my goals and plans are with regards to everything, and how I am going to obtain those goals.

My main aim is to prove the existence of spirits, a lot of individuals will go at this in order to prove that spirits do not exist, however I wish to be the opposite, I am wanting to find a way to show evidence that can be repeated over and over again, it is no good just for example taking that one photo above, and saying "hey look, spirits do exist as I took a photo". On the other hand, if I could say here, look, every time I take a photo, I catch a spirit, then it is repeatable evidence, meaning that I can do the same thing again and again.

If we take that photo above for example, the one I took during the ghost hunt, yes it looks a great photo, and yes it could be called a spirit, but without being able to do the same thing again, its my word against others, and one photo is not really proof. I see photos of god, all over the place, but it is not something that someone can just go and do, you cannot take a camera and photo god. Thus the evidence is not enough. I want to be able to give you the camera, and say here take a photo, and bang, you capture a spirit.

For that reason, we really have to understand how my theories work, and what we can do to prove my theories. During this book, I have provided hints as to ways that we could or could not prove what I believe, and during this chapter I am going to elaborate on my ideas. So please bear with me.

High Speed Camera's

During this book, I have already explained how our bodies can only distinguish around 250 frames per second, in vision, however if we consider that spirits (if we use the timing above) can appear in any of 5 million ticks during that second, the chances of us seeing them are very slim, This I believe is where high speed cameras, could provide a great deal of advantage to us. The selection in the image above, have the ability to reach around 200,000 images per

second. Taking that into consideration, we would reduce the chances of seeing a spirit from 1 in 20,000 to 1 in 25.
With a 1 in 25% chance of seeing a spirit (based only on the direction) we have dramatically reduced the chance, and given us a great advantage.

If we take into consideration, all the other factors that I have already covered in this book, which resulted in a 3400 trillion to one chance, we reduce that down to a little more manageable 1 in 1.7 billion. Still extreme odds I know, but much more manageable.

Now there are camera's that can record at 1 million frames per second and they would result in a ratio of 1 in 5 just based on direction and a 1 in 300 million based on all the different potential aspects, 1 in 300 million is much better odds than what we currently have available.

The problem with this of course, lies in the cost of these devices, a typical 2-3 thousand images per second high speed camera, can cost in excess of £10,000, as such it will be a long time before I can manage to obtain one of these great devices. As soon as I can I will, and hopefully be able to catch more paranormal spirits on video.

Ultra Sonic Recording

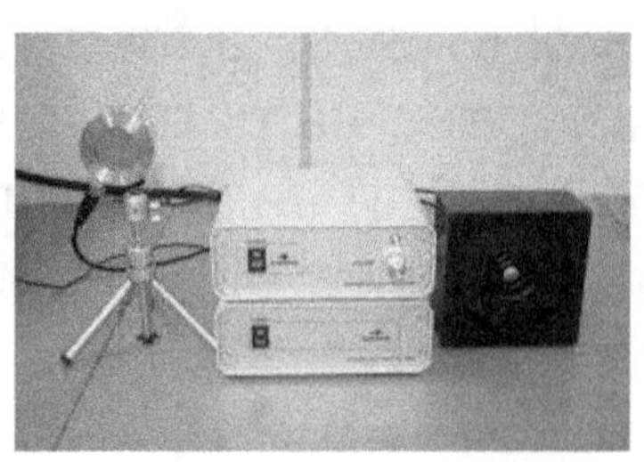

As we have already discussed in this book, we know that some children can hear spirits, and we believe animals can hear spirits, so the question is why.

Medical experts have discovered that children can actually hear at a higher frequency than adults, as well as that dogs can to, so it can be assumed that spirits communicate at frequency that is much higher than the human ear can work with, as such Ultra Sonic.
An Ultra Sonic recorder, will allow its user to record sounds that are beyond human hearing, and also allow you to replay those sounds back at a more reasonable frequency allowing for us to hear them.

I can see the question you are asking now, how do I know that spirits communicate ultrasonically, and not sub sonic. And the answer I can give to this is I don't, however, I can use science.

Let me explain, for sound waves to travel and for us to hear them, we manipulate wind, our breathing, the sound waves carry through the air because of the pressure or lack of pressure we build through our voice box as 3rd dimensional beings.

Now, a spirit on the other hand does not have a physical body and as such cannot push air through the voice box in order to speak. As such they do not produce the sound waves that we can hear, as it requires wind pressure.

Saying this however, it is possible to create a sound wave with no breathing or forcing air through something, by simple closing or opening something, for example drop something next to a feather, it doesn't breath but it will blow enough air to create a breeze that will move the feather, we can move it further by blowing on it.

Assuming that a spirit can actually use its voice box, without pushing air out of it, then it could create small waves, just like the object we drop. And the smaller the wave, the higher the frequency, as such spirits if able to speak, would speak in a frequency we could not hear, as for us to hear we would need air waves.

Again, I am looking to purchase a good quality Ultra Sonic Recorder, one that can record a huge range of frequencies.

Electronics

One of my many hobbies are electronics, and I hope to put that to great use, my plans include building a couple of my own instruments which can be used within the field of the paranormal, including a form of radio, that only works on the higher waves, and not the radio waves. As I have already explained if a spirit actually speak within the Ultra Sonic area of sound, then It may be possible to create a device like a radio that can pick up that ultra sonic vibration and translate them into a sound we can hear, Much like the devices above. However this would in comparison to them items, be such a simple device that my expectations would not be high.

I would also like to create another form of EMF device, one that you can actually use to pinpoint the actual cause of the field. Imagine if you will the device the ghost busters used, with two arms protruding from it, now imagine if the device had several EMF sensors and each one was read and using electronics and programming, we could create a small interface that would allow you to pinpoint the location of the field. A small screen would after calculations show exactly where the field was emanating from. Much like a sonar system.

Other items that I believe may be useful, is sonar and radar systems, although I'm not 100% faithful that these devices would be any good, it would be worth trying them out.

Location, Location, Location

One final point I want to make, is that my experiments will mean nothing if we don't have a great location in order to run them, Unfortunately I find and believe that a lot of the locations, where ghost hunts are held, are not actually paranormally active, and that stories are manifested from people who actually don't know exactly what they are doing, Hear a creak, its paranormal, hear a bang its paranormal, and as such these places suddenly become a breeding ground for entertainment rather than research.

For this reason, I am planning on solely proprietor my time on properties that actually have someone who can actually state they have witnessed paranormal activity rather than places that have a history. As we all know, history can and is manipulated in order to be good for the viewer.

Private Residence

Of all the paranormal activity I have dealt with in the past, the most prominent and regular is when I am asleep, as such whenever possible I would like to spend a few nights at a location that claims to have paranormal activity, recording both the sound and video for the entire evening. Of course in the past when this has been happening I have not had the technology available to enable me to record the evening. I believe with the right equipment, the results may actually be pleasing.

CHAPTER FOURTEEN
How you can help

Although my plans are very simple to understand, there is unfortunately no way that I can accomplish them at the moment, due to funding issues, and the price of the equipment that is required. However if you are someone who is interested in this sort of thing, and you are looking for the possibilities of a partnership/funding, then I would love to speak with you.

If you are a company who produces any of this equipment and are interesting in assisting me with my experiments, then again please feel free to give me a shout, I would be happy to discuss the potential of a co operative agreement of some sort.

I am more than happy to work in a partnership, as my interest is in proving the existence of spirits, not making a name for myself, however, if my theories are correct, then I suppose the later will be a result of this research.

If you wish to contact me you can do so on the following email address

admin@applebeez.org

I do want to add, that I have recently joined a group called "East Durham Paranormal Research Group" who are dedicated to research, rather than entertainment, you can find our website at the following address

http://www.eastdurhamparanormalgr.co.uk

We will be documenting our research on the website, and also on the YouTube channel which has been set up. Feel free to contact us or even visit the website and YouTube channel to keep up to date with our progress.

CHAPTER FIFTEEN
References

All images portrayed in this book are either my own or public domain images, retrieved from the following sites, all images are free for personal or business use.

Needpix.com
Pxhere.com
hdqwalls.com
Publicdomainpictures.net
www.pickpik.com
Pixabay.com

The following websites and you tube videos have also been referenced in this book:

Jeff Dunham
https://www.youtube.com/watch?v=dO5m9sabh7k&t=140s

Children who remember past lives search result:

https://www.youtube.com/results?
search_query=children+remember+past+lives